Horses of America

DOROTHY HINSHAW PATENT

INTERNATIONAL ARABIAN HORSE ASSOCIATION

Holiday House, New York

For Bill and Sandy

Acknowledgments

I wish to thank the following people for taking time to share their horses and their knowledge with me: Mr. and Mrs. Joel Gleason, Gleason Quarter Horses; Jane Spahr, Ravenwood Ranch Arabians; Charlie Yerian, Belgians; Fred Hartkorn, POAs; Earl Liebig, American Saddlebreds; The Willard Crockett family, Crockett's Clydesdales; Lana and Jack Grady, Totem Peaks Morgans; Glen and Jill Parker, Tennessee Walking Horses; Pearl Tompkins, Tennessee Walking Horses; Dale Bagnell, Bagnell's Stables, Quarter Horses, Thoroughbreds, Paints; Forrest Davis, San Francisco Ranch, Belgians; Doug Hammill, Clydesdales; Jim Cole, Cowboy Polo; Jessie and John Ralston, Jumping Horses; Arthur Jenson, Shetland Ponies; The Ray R. Miller family, Miller's KN Ranch, Percherons and Shetland Ponies.

The following people were kind enough to allow us to use photos of them and/or their horses: René Johnshoy, p. 5; Bob Morin, Mission Arabians, pp. 13, 14; Jane Spahr, pp. 16, 17; Lana and Jack Grady, pp. 22, 24; Earl Liebig (trainer), p. 27; Glen and Jill Parker, p. 28; Bill Crockett, p. 36; Willard Crockett, p. 38; Ed Ernst, p. 40; Forrest Davis, p. 41; Hope Litzinger and Joey Hurt, p. 42; Sandy and Bill Munoz, p. 47; Jane and Cary Spahr, p. 48; Dale Bagnell, p. 50; Debbie Chapman, p. 51; Fred Hartkorn, p. 59; Marilyn Stacy, p. 74.

Library of Congress Cataloging in Publication Data

Patent, Dorothy Hinshaw.
 Horses of America.

 Summary: Discusses the evolution and characteristics
of various breeds of horses and identifies breeds for
work, sports, and pleasure, and those that are "all-
around" horses.

 1. Horses—America—Juvenile literature. 2. Horse
breeds—America—Juvenile literature. [1. Horses.
2. Horse breeds] I. Title.
SF284.A6P37   636.1'00973   81-4165
ISBN 0-8234-0399-8   AACR2

Contents

CHAPTER ONE
Horses in America

Horses have been important in America since early days. Horses helped the Spanish explorers search for gold. They helped the Spanish missionaries settle the southwest. They plowed fields for early settlers in the east and for later settlers as Americans moved west. They helped clear the forests by dragging logs, and they pulled buggies for people on their trips to town. Horses changed the lives of the Indians and made the life of the cattle rancher possible.

People have always had special feelings for horses aside from their usefulness. All through their years of working together, horses and humans have also been friends. Even when automobiles and tractors came along, many people still valued horses. Some used them for pleasure, riding them in parks or racing them. Others used them for work, preferring the quiet friendship of horses to the noisiness of machines.

Today, many horses still work for people. Cowboys use horses to herd cattle. Many farmers use horses to

René Johnshoy and her horse Skybird enjoy competing together and winning blue ribbons. BILL MUNOZ

plow their fields. Loggers use horses in the deep woods and on steep slopes where machines would ruin the land. And people love to see a good horse race, jumping contest, or polo match.

The Earliest Horses

The horse is truly an American animal. It evolved here long ago, from a prehistoric animal called *Eohippus.* Eohippus was very different from horses. It was so small that it would only come up to the knee of a modern horse. It had several toes on each foot instead of one hoof. It had a short neck and a rounded back. Over a period of 50 million years, the changes occurred which led from Eohippus to the horse. Those changes took place in the area that is now the Rocky Mountains of the United States. From there, horses spread to South America, Europe, and Asia.

Then, about 10,000 years ago, horses completely died out in America. No one is quite sure how this happened. Perhaps a terrible disease killed all of them. Or maybe the first people to settle in America killed them off for food. But whatever happened, there were no horses in America for thousands of years. The American Indians knew nothing about horses since they had never seen them. The Indians had to walk wherever they went. They used dogs to help them drag sleds which carried their belongings.

Horses Come Back

Spanish explorers brought horses with them when they came to America. The very first were twenty-five Spanish horses which came with Christopher Columbus on his second voyage in 1493. From then on, horses came with every Spanish ship to the New World. The Spaniards needed them for exploring and for warring with the Indians. The sight of a man on top of a horse was very frightening and confusing to the Indians. They had never seen anything like it before. A soldier on a horse had a tremendous advantage over an Indian on foot. Horses made the conquistadors' job much easier.

The long voyage across the Atlantic Ocean was hard on the horses. They were hung in hammocks on the deck of the ship so that they wouldn't be thrown overboard during storms. Day after day they hung there, swaying back and forth gently with the waves. Half the horses commonly died. Those that survived were quite weak after two or three months without exercise. But when they arrived on shore, they had to go right to work, carrying men and supplies on their backs.

The Spanish realized just how important horses were. They always brought both stallions and mares with them, even though they only rode the stallions. The mares were used for breeding. By 1500, the Spanish government already had a ranch with 60 brood mares set up on the island of Hispaniola.

This Plains Indian is riding a pinto, which was favored by the Indians because its spotted coat blended with the background.
COURTESY OF THE AMERICAN MUSEUM OF NATURAL HISTORY

Horses in the Early West

During the next 200 years, the Spanish explored and settled much of the American southwest and west. Horses helped them do it. The missionaries came to

.8.

teach the Indians and to settle the land. At first, the Indians were not allowed to ride horses. The Spanish were afraid of what would happen if the Indians learned how to use horses in war. But as time passed, the missionaries needed help managing their herds. There were not enough settlers to do the work. So they had to teach the Indians how to ride horses. The Indians adapted very quickly. Indians who were unfriendly to the settlers learned about horses, too, and rapidly became expert horsemen. They figured out how to use horses to hunt buffalo and how to use them in war. Horses soon were a vital part of the Indians' lives.

Horses made it possible for the Indians to resist the white settlers who came from the east as well as the Spanish. An expert Comanche warrior could slide down on one side of his horse so that only the very bottom of his moccasin could be seen peeking over the top. In this position, with his whole body hidden and protected by his mount, the Indian could shoot arrows at his enemies from under the horse's neck.

Wild Horses

The Spanish settlers didn't build fences around their lands, and many horses escaped from them. Horses also escaped when Indians raided the settlers' herds and stampeded them off. By the end of the 17th century,

Wild mustangs still survive in a few western states. BUREAU OF
LAND MANAGEMENT

there were wild horses all over the west and as far north
as the Canadian border. These horses, called mustangs,
were often captured and broken by settlers, Indians, and
cowboys. They were a very important source of cheap
horseflesh for such early Americans.

There are still mustangs in the west. Some of their
ancestors were Spanish and Indian horses. Others were
plow horses and riding horses that escaped later from
farms and ranches. Many present-day ranchers want to
get rid of all the wild horses. They say the horses compete
for food with cattle and wild game animals. But some
other people like the wild horses. They say the horses are
a part of western history and deserve to survive. Three

areas in the west have been set aside for the wild horses—the Pryor Mountain Wild Horse Range near the Montana-Wyoming border, the Nellis Bombing Range in Nevada, and the Little Book Cliffs Wild Horse Range in Colorado.

But wild horses also live in other parts of the west. Sometimes the government decides that the horses must be removed to make room for cattle and game animals. Other times the herds on the wild horse ranges must be thinned out. Then the horses are rounded up by cowboys and helicopters. The horses are given to people who want to provide them with homes. This government plan is called the Adopt a Wild Horse Program. If someone wants to adopt a wild horse, he or she can apply by writing to the Bureau of Land Management, U.S. Government. The person must provide the horse with a proper home. If it is well cared for, the person can become the legal owner of the horse after one year.

Taming the East

While the horses were helping the Spanish and the Indians in the west, they were working for the early settlers in the east. Most of the horses in the east were also of Spanish origin. Many of them were captured from wild herds, just as in the west. A few horses were also brought over from England and the Netherlands. The first truly American breeds began with small, tough horses. They were caught and tamed by the colonists or bought by them from the Indians. Some tribes, such as the Chickasaw, were famous for their fine horses. These animals were small, only 13 to 14 hands high. (A horse's height is measured in units called "hands." One hand is equal to 4 inches. The height is always taken from the ground to the top of the withers. If a horse is said to be 15.2 hands high, that means that it is 15 hands and 2 inches—62 inches—tall at the withers).

Horse racing was already popular among the colonists in 1690. Usually the only straight, smooth stretch of road was the main street of town, so races were run there. Because the street was short, the races were short. Not very many horses could run at the same time, down the narrow street. Therefore only two or three ran at one time. It wasn't long before this contest was a match race between two horses running a quarter mile. A fast horse which could win these races was considered quite valuable. These "short horses" could get a quick start and run very fast for a short distance. They were the first American "Quarter Horses."

Horses in America Today

There are dozens of horse breeds in the world. Only a few horses of some breeds live in the United States. Other kinds, because they are popular, live here in

Raising horses such as these Arabians is still a popular activity in the United States. BILL MUNOZ

larger numbers. Several popular breeds, like the Quarter Horse, actually originated in America. The Arabian, on the other hand, came here from another part of the world.

For each horse breed, there is an association which keeps track and makes rules for it. A purebred horse must be listed with the breed association to be officially a member of that breed. Some horses are bred for special uses such as racing or farming. Others are used for many different purposes. Let's take a look at some of the most popular horse breeds and types in the United States to see what part horses play in our lives today.

.13.

CHAPTER TWO
All-Around Horses

For most people, the best horse is the one that can be used to fill many different needs. An all-purpose horse can help out with the chores, pull a sleigh in winter, and be a fine riding companion. Most horse breeds are like that, and America has produced several which can meet the needs of just about anyone. Only one popular, all-purpose breed, the Arabian, actually came from somewhere else. All the rest were developed here in America to meet the needs of a new country.

These young Arabians may end up as pleasure horses, show animals, cow ponies, or jumpers. BILL MUNOZ

The classic Arabian head has a dished face, large eyes, and wide nostrils. BILL MUNOZ

The Arabian

The Arabian is the oldest pure breed of horse. Some Arabian ancestry is found in just about all light horse breeds. Arabian horses are bred all over the world, but they originated in the deserts of the Middle East many centuries ago. The horse was vital to the wandering tribes of the Arabian deserts. The people had to travel long distances, and their horses helped them to travel quickly. In those days, the Arabian's horse was so valued that it was treated as a part of the family. Mares were preferred as riding horses since they were gentler than stallions. They were less likely to whinny when another horse approached, giving away their location to an enemy. The mare slept right in the tent with her owner and acted as watchdog as well as a mount. Even today, owners of Arabians say that their horses enjoy the company of people more than most horses do.

The Arabian is a beautiful, small horse (14.1 to 15.1 hands), but it makes up in strength and spirit what it lacks in size. Arabians have long, silky manes and tails; graceful, arched necks; and small heads with wide nostrils, small ears, and big eyes. The Arabian is famous for its "dished face." While most horses have a straight

Arabian horses love to run in the pasture. BILL MUNOZ

profile, the classic Arabian face is slightly curved inward below the eyes.

Arabians are very alert horses, always curious about their surroundings. They are famous for their high spirits and will set off running in the pasture at the slightest excuse. It takes skill to train an Arabian since these horses do not like to be bossed around. They respond better to gentleness and patience.

Arabians can be trained for almost any purpose. They are used for running races because of their speed. They are very popular for long trail rides because of their stamina. They make good cattle horses because of their alertness. They are often fine jumpers because they have strong leg bones.

Many people think that Arabians are too spirited for children. However, some Arabians, even stallions, are used by experienced young riders in horse shows and in trail riding competitions.

The Quarter Horse is a strong, stocky animal. LYNN BARLOTTA

The American Quarter Horse

The Quarter Horse is the most popular horse in the world. There are over a million-and-a-half horses listed in the official American registry. Since its start as a quarter-mile racer in the early colonies, the Quarter Horse has developed into a horse with many uses. Quarter Horses are popular as family riding horses since they are usually gentle and calm. A Quarter Horse can be trained to follow the commands of its rider, which makes it a good pleasure horse. It can also be trained to use its mind, which is important in handling cattle.

.19.

The Quarter Horse is a medium-sized animal, from 14.3 to 16 hands high. It has a nice head with small ears and large jaws. Its body is solid, with a short back, deep chest, and fairly short legs. The Quarter Horse is famous for its strong, sturdy muscles. All these traits make the Quarter Horse a good cow horse. In fact, in the early west, the modern Quarter Horse was bred more as a cow horse than as a racer. Its compact body allows it to maneuver quickly to control cattle. Its strong muscles give it the power to pull back on a roped steer while a cowboy wrestles the steer to the ground. Quarter Horses are still fast over short distances. They can outrun any cattle which try to escape from the herd.

In recent years, to increase their speed in races, Quarter Horses have been bred with Thoroughbreds. The offspring are not as chunky as a typical Quarter Horse and are more suited to racing than to working with cattle.

The Quarter Horse talent for "stopping on a dime" is tested in horse shows. BILL MUNOZ

The Morgan is a small, strong horse with a thick, flowing mane and tail. BILL MUNOZ

.22.

The Morgan Horse

In the late 1700s, a very special horse named Figure was owned by a poor Vermont singing teacher named Justin Morgan. No one knows exactly where he came from, but Figure was a small, powerful stallion. He could pull more weight than a bigger horse, and he could run faster than many racers. He could work long hours and still be fresh for a ride into town or for a race. He was truly an amazing animal. Justin Morgan earned a bit of extra cash by renting his horse to local loggers and farmers, and the horse's fame spread. When Mr. Morgan died in 1798, his horse passed from owner to owner and was often mistreated. But he still worked hard for people. Now he was called "Justin Morgan," after his early owner. He is the only horse to have an entire breed named after him.

Luckily, Figure could pass his remarkable traits on to his offspring. Like him, they were strong animals that could move quickly. They could work for a long time without getting tired. During the history of America, the Morgan Horse has been used for just about every sort of work that horses can do. Morgans have pulled plows, dragged logs, won races, pulled buggies, and carried their owners on their backs for mile after mile.

Today there are more than 30,000 registered Morgan Horses. They are somewhat small (14.1 to 15.2

hands) and are usually dark in color, with few white markings. Morgans have thick, beautiful, flowing manes and tails. Their legs are strong, and they have powerful, arched necks. Many Morgans lift their hooves high off the ground as they trot. This makes them popular for pulling buggies. They are also very good for trail riding and make fine, all-around pleasure horses.

The Morgan Horse has an especially powerful, arched neck. BILL MUNOZ

.24.

The American Saddlebred

The tall and graceful American Saddlebred is an elegant horse. It used to be the mount of the Kentucky plantation owner. It carried its owner around all day while he surveyed his fields.

The breed was developed by crossing Arabians, Thoroughbreds, Morgans, and pacers. Today, it looks quite different from any of the breeds it came from. Long and lean might be the best way to describe this beautiful horse. Its legs and neck are long and slim, and its mane and tail are thick and flowing. Its head is topped with delicate pointed ears which prick forward in a friendly way when you approach.

Saddlebreds can be trained to perform two unique gaits. These are called the slow gait and the rack. Both are called "man-made" gaits since the horses do not do them naturally. They must learn how to from a trainer. In either gait, only one hoof hits the ground at a time. The horse lifts its feet very high, moving each leg in a circle as it steps. The rack is tiring for the horse but very comfortable for the rider.

For many years, Saddlebreds were raised and trained mainly for the show-ring. The horse's tail was set in a leather brace which held the tail up high. Before the show, the brace was removed. Then ginger, which stings, was placed under the tail to keep it high. Heavy, padded

When the Saddlebred does the rack, it puts its feet down one at a time in rapid succession. HOWARD SKAGGS

shoes and chains were used to make the horse lift its legs higher during training.

These practices still take place, but more and more people are getting away from them. The Saddlebred is also becoming more popular as a pleasure horse than it used to be. Because it is gentle and willing to learn, this breed can be trained to do almost any job. It is being used for jumping, trail riding, polo, and even ranch work.

This elegant American Saddlebred, nicknamed "Hotshot," is fiery in the show-ring but peaceful and gentle at home. The small chains on his hind legs encourage him to lift up his feet when moving but do not seem to bother him. BILL MUNOZ

The Tennessee Walking Horse

Like the Saddlebred, the Tennessee Walking Horse was originally used by plantation owners. It was developed from the same breeds as the American Saddlebred. But even so, the Tennessee Walker looks different from the Saddlebred. It is more powerful looking and is not as tall and thin.

The long stride of the Tennessee Walking Horse allows it to walk faster than some horses trot. This mare in her shaggy winter coat shows the natural walk rather than the exaggerated show-ring gait. BILL MUNOZ

The Tennessee Walking Horse has a unique gait called the running walk, which allows it to cover many miles quickly and easily. This special walk comes naturally to it. Even young foals in the pasture use it. The running walk is very comfortable for the rider. The horse moves gracefully, lifting its front feet high and reaching its hind feet several inches in front of where the front feet were set down. This easy gait is so fast that the Walker leaves other breeds far behind.

Like Saddlebreds, Walkers were first mostly bred and trained for show. Their hooves were allowed to grow very long. Heavy shoes with thick pads under them were used on their feet. Their tails were cut so that they were always held up high.

Many horses are still trained in these ways for shows. But more and more people are enjoying the Tennessee Walking Horse as a pleasure animal. The fast, comfortable Walker gaits are perfect for long rides. And because it's very gentle, the Walker is a good family horse.

Thoroughbred brood mares enjoy life in the pasture in West Virginia. USDA PHOTO BY AL BEATY

CHAPTER THREE
Flashy and Fast

People have probably raced horses as long as they've had them. The spirit of competition—my animal is better than yours—has always been with us. We know that the ancient Persians raced horse-drawn chariots. And other people of long ago must have raced on horseback. In the United States today, there are several sorts of horse racing. There are short races for Quarter Horses and longer races for Thoroughbreds, trotters, and pacers. The even longer races for steeplechasers include challenging jumps. Racing is popular at county and state fairs as well as at the big tracks. Few people realize how popular Quarter Horse racing is today and how much money it involves. The richest race in the world, held in New Mexico on Labor Day, is for Quarter Horses. The total prize money is around one million dollars. The winner takes home about three times as much as the Kentucky Derby champion, and the whole race is over in less than twenty-five seconds.

Racing played an important part along with cattle ranching in Quarter Horse history. But two breeds—the Thoroughbred and the Standardbred—were developed *only* because of racing.

Rockhill Native shows that the long forward reach of the back hooves is part of the Thoroughbred's famous stride. PHOTO COMMUNICATIONS

The Thoroughbred

Like the Arabian, the Thoroughbred is found all over the world. And also like the Arabian, this big, strong horse has been used to improve many of the world's horses.

The Thoroughbred was first developed in Great Britain, where flat racing (racing without jumps) was popular. About 300 years ago, Arabian, Turkish, and

Barb stallions were brought to Britain and bred with English mares to produce faster racers. Three of these stallions gave rise to such fine colts that all Thoroughbreds today can be traced back to them.

Thoroughbreds have been very popular in the United States. American thoroughbreds hold many world speed records. They have been bred to mature early, since the best-known American races are for two- and three-year-olds. The official birthday of every American Thoroughbred is January 1, even if it is born in May. A Thoroughbred may have a rider on its back when it is barely over a year old. Horses of most breeds are often not ridden until after their second birthday.

Thoroughbreds are usually big horses, averaging over 16 hands high. Although their nervousness and high spirits make them ideal racers, they are often used for other purposes. Many Thoroughbreds are fine jumpers and polo ponies. And many which are not fast enough for the racetrack end up as well-loved pleasure horses.

The Standardbred

The Standardbred is the greatest trotter in the world. It was developed here in the United States. When breeders from other countries want to improve their trotting horses, they breed them to American Standardbreds. Almost all Standardbreds can be traced back to one

Two Standardbreds, a trotter and a pacer, go around the track. The trotter is on the left, the pacer on the right. HERB BYERS, INTERNATIONAL MUSEUM OF THE HORSE

great Thoroughbred stallion named Messenger. Messenger came to America from England in 1788. Although he never entered a trotting race, he produced many fine trotters as well as runners.

In general, the Standardbred is less nervous than the Thoroughbred. It is also smaller and has a heavier body and heavier legs. Often the rump of a Standardbred is higher than its withers. One reason the Standardbred trots so fast is because of the length of its stride. When a Standardbred trots, its hind feet reach much farther forward than do those of other breeds.

Trotting races became popular in New England in the early 1800s. But until 1830, most trotting races were run with a rider on the horse. Today, Standardbred races (called harness races) are run with the horses pulling lightweight carts called sulkies.

Nowadays, Standardbreds are raced as pacers as well as trotters. A trotter puts down the right front foot and the left rear foot at the same time, and the left front and rear right feet at the same time. A pacer moves the two legs on one side together instead. Pacing is slightly faster than trotting, and today pacing races are more popular than trotting races.

Bill Crockett of Victor, Montana, uses his Clydesdales to work his farm. HOWARD SKAGGS

CHAPTER FOUR
Powerful Workers

Draft horses were once a vital part of American farming. Before trucks and tractors, horses pulled the plows and hauled the loads on the farm. But when machines came along, many farmers sold their horses and turned to machines. The number of draft horses in the United States dropped trememdously, and some people feared they would die out altogether. But many true horse lovers hung onto their heavy horses. They continued to use them for plowing the land, dragging logs, and pulling the hay wagon.

Recently, people have become interested in small family farms. Gas and machinery prices have gone way up, and draft horses are again becoming popular. In 1952, only 671 Belgian horse foals were registered in the United States. But in 1980, around 3,200 were registered. It now looks as if the draft horse is here to stay.

Originally draft horses were not used to pull heavy loads. They carried them instead. They were the mounts of the medieval knights. The knights wore heavy metal suits of armor, and so did the horses. Often the animal had to carry over 700 pounds, so the horses had to be big and strong.

Draft horses can be very large. They are sometimes over 18 hands high and weigh more than a ton. Their hooves may be as big as dinner plates. Fortunately, draft horses are peaceful, gentle animals. They are quite willing to devote their strength to helping humans.

Draft horses are sometimes used for other than ordinary farm work. After the harvest is in, the farmer may saddle up his Belgian and ride it out to hunt game. In Kansas, draft horses are used to separate fattened cattle from the stockyard herds. The horses move the steers slowly and gently so they don't lose weight. In Japan, Percherons are actually raced. They pull heavy iron sleds with drivers over a 220-yard course of sand hills.

Five sorts of draft horses are used in the United States—Shires, Suffolks, Clydesdales, Percherons, and Belgians. The first two breeds are quite rare, however.

Clydesdales

The Clydesdale came from Scotland in the region around the river Clyde. These horses are the most familiar draft horses in the United States. This is probably because of a famous show called the Anheuser-Busch Clydesdale hitch. The company has two teams of eight 18-hand bay geldings. Each horse has four white stockings, a white blaze, and a black mane and tail. These beautiful horses make over 300 appearances each year, showing their style and strength to people everywhere.

Clydesdales are classy horses. They have long, feathered, white legs which they lift proudly with every step. Clydes have big, powerful shoulders and strong, arched necks. They are usually brown or bay in color, but blacks, roans, chestnuts, and grays are also found.

These Clydesdales are taking it easy in their corral. BILL MUNOZ

This powerful gray Percheron and his companion work from sun-up to sundown as logging horses in Montana forests. BILL MUNOZ

Percherons

Percherons come from the La Perche district of northern France. They are the only draft horses which have a dash of Arabian blood. This gives them a special, refined beauty. Percherons are born black, but many turn gray as they grow up. Nine out of ten Percherons are either black or gray.

Percherons are light of foot despite their size. They move quickly and can turn around in a small area. Because of their strength and agility, Percherons were used during the Civil War to pull heavy cannons. After the war, they became popular as work horses in the south because they could stand the hot, humid summer weather. Percherons lift their feet high when trotting, which makes them flashy show horses.

Belgians

The Belgian is the most popular draft horse in the United States today. Belgians are handsome animals, with their sturdy bodies and thick manes and tails. Belgians are often sorrel colored, with light manes and tails and light stockings. They look much like giant, dark palominos.

Belgians are very strong and hold the world's weight-pulling record. The stallions often weigh more than a ton, and the heaviest horse in the world was a Belgian. His name was Brooklyn Supreme. He stood 19.2 hands and weighed 3,200 pounds. It took a 30-inch piece of iron to make just one shoe for him.

Belgians do all the work on The San Francisco Ranch in Polson, Montana. BILL MUNOZ

.42.

CHAPTER FIVE
Color Counts

Horses come in many colors—chestnut, bay, white, spotted, and so forth. Certain breeds may tend to show certain colors. For example, most Percherons are black or gray. But usually color is not a trait of the breed.

Some horse color patterns are especially popular with people. Golden palominos, colorful pintos, and pure white horses stand out in a crowd. Because people like these and some other colors so much, special organizations exist to register them. But these color patterns are not the same as true breeds. A "registered buckskin," for example, may be a Quarter Horse, an Arabian, or a mixed breed. Some of the color registries have rules about which breeds can be registered. Draft horses are often excluded, for instance. But none allow only one breed to be registered.

The strong legs and feet of the Appaloosa make it a good jumper. This horse shows the mottled skin on its face, which is an Appaloosa characteristic. BILL MUNOZ

The Appaloosa

Spotted horses have been known since ancient times. But the modern Appaloosa is truly an American horse. It originated with the Nez Perce Indians of Idaho, Washington, and Montana. The name "Appaloosa" comes from the Palouse River. Along its banks, the Nez Perce raised their famous spotted horses. The Indians chose these horses carefully, using only the best for breeding purposes. Their horses were famous for their colorful, spotted coats and for their speed and stamina. The land where they lived was quite dry with little for horses to eat. Even today, old-fashioned Appaloosas are known as "easy keepers." They require less food than most other horses.

Appaloosas have strong legs and hooves and can be used for many things. The Appaloosa makes a good cow horse since it was bred as a buffalo hunter by the Indians. It also makes a good pleasure horse since its walk is fast and comfortable.

Several traits set the Appaloosa apart from other horses. All Appaloosas have a light-and-dark pattern, especially on the face. The eye of most horses is completely dark. But Appaloosas have a white area, or sclera, around the dark iris, just as people do. This gives the horse a somewhat "wild-eyed" look that has nothing to do with the animal's spirit. The hooves of Appaloosas

The old-fashioned western Appaloosa is a gentle horse. BILL
MUNOZ

are usually striped up and down with dark and light. Most of the time, a large area of the body is one color, while the rear part is white with irregular spots. Some Appaloosas are white with spots all over their bodies. A few are dark with white spots. The mane and tail on an Appaloosa tend to be thin and wispy.

Some modern Appaloosas are quite beautiful since horses from several breeds can be registered as Appaloosas if they show the proper coloring. But the western Appaloosa, descended from the Indian horses, is often quite homely looking with its spotty skin and thin mane and tail. Whether they are pretty or not, the old-fashioned horses are usually gentle and good with children.

.45.

The Buckskin

Buckskin is one of the original color patterns shown by primitive horses. A buckskin has a body in some shade of yellow, ranging from pale gold to almost brown. The lower legs, mane, and tail are black or dark brown. To be registered as a buckskin, a horse needs to show only these traits. But the preferred buckskin also sports a dark stripe down its back and may have another stripe running across its shoulders from side to side. The black on its legs breaks up into "tiger stripes" near the knees.

The powerful Quarter Horse muscles are at work in this buckskin. Part of the dark stripe down the back can be seen, along with the dark mane, tail, and legs. PHOTO BY GARY LAKE

Suzie will grow up to be a beautiful golden palomino. BILL MUNOZ

The Palomino

Some people think the palomino is the most beautiful of all horses. It has a golden body with a white or almost white mane and tail. Some palominos are so light in color that their bodies are almost white. Others are so dark that they are close to brown. Palominos have always been popular as parade horses because of their good looks. People have tried and tried to get palominos to become a breed, but this hasn't worked. When two palominos are bred together, only half the foals are palominos.

Pinto and Paint

To many people, the pinto "pony" is the Indian pony. We picture an Indian with a feathered headdress riding a black-and-white pony bareback. Pintos were popular with the Indians because their patches of white and brown or black broke up their outline. This made them harder for enemies to see.

For many years, pintos were thought to be lower in quality than other horses. Even today, many breed associations refuse to register them.

But recently, these colorful horses have become more popular. Pintos of any breed can be registered with The Pinto Horse Association. The American Paint Horse Association, however, will register only pintos with Quarter Horse and Thoroughbred breeding. The Paint Horse is thought of as a "stock horse," used generally in the same ways as Quarter Horses.

This pinto mare always has a pinto foal. While she is mostly white, her foal is mostly brown. BILL MUNOZ

This beautiful American Paint stallion has the powerful build of a good stock horse. BILL MUNOZ

This blue-eyed American White Horse squints in the bright sunlight. BILL MUNOZ

The American White Horse

White horses have always been thought of as special. In many societies, white horses were favorites of royalty. In the United States today, certain white horses can be registered with the American White Horse Association. These horses are born white. They have white hair, pink skin, and blue, brown, or hazel eyes. They were once called American Albinos. That name was confusing, for true albinos have pink eyes, and there are no true albino horses. White horses are in demand with groups that want to have matched animals. They are also popular with circuses.

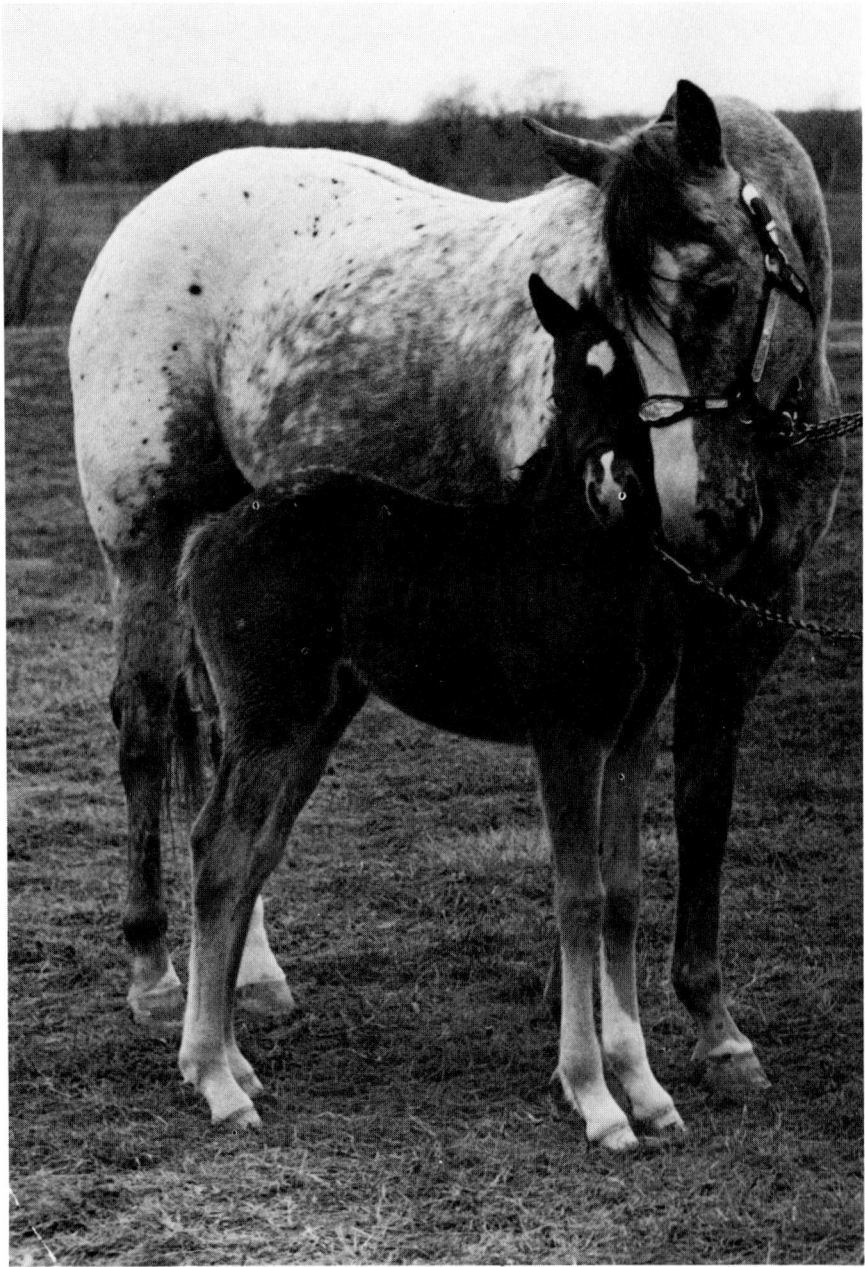

CHAPTER SIX
Ponies Are Horses Too

Horses smaller than 14.2 hands are called ponies. Some ponies are just small horses, but others are members of definite breeds. There are many pony breeds, and several are used in the United States. The Hackney Pony is a very classy animal, used as a harness pony rather than for riding. Hackneys lift their hooves way up when they trot. The Connemara Pony from Ireland is becoming popular in the United States, especially for jumping events. But the three most popular ponies in America are the Shetland, the Welsh, and the Pony of the Americas.

A Pony of the Americas mare nuzzles her foal. COURTESY OF THE PONY OF THE AMERICAS CLUB

The Shetland Pony

Shetlands are the most familiar ponies. They are also the smallest breed, being no taller than 11.2 hands. They came from the Shetland Islands off the coast of Scotland. They lived there half wild for centuries. Island Shetlands are rugged animals, with shaggy winter coats, thick necks, and very broad backs. They look almost like miniature draft horses. Their small size and heavy build made them ideal for work in coal mines. Small children were once used on the Shetland Islands to carry coal from the mines. But in 1840, a law was passed forbidding the use of women and children in the mines. The small but powerful Shetland took over their jobs.

Today, Shetlands in the United States come in two very different types. One is much like the original island pony, with a stocky build and broad back. These animals are only about 9.2 hands high and can be ridden just by small children. They are sometimes quite stubborn and may be hard for a child to handle.

The other sort of Shetland is called the American Shetland. This animal is totally different from the island-type pony. In the early 20th century, many Shetlands were brought to the United States. Here they were not needed as work ponies. They were used for pleasure instead, so breeders looked for different traits from those of the island ponies. They looked for longer legs.

The Island-type Shetland Pony has a barrel-shaped body and a thick forelock and mane. ALAN J. KANIA

They bred for slimmer necks and leaner bodies. Sometimes Hackney Ponies were bred with Shetlands to get the desired, more refined look. The result is the American Shetland, which is a high stepping, high-strung show pony. American Shetlands are rarely ridden but are driven in harness. Trainers let the ponies' hooves grow long and put on heavily weighted shoes to get the animals to lift their legs high. A purebred pony from the Shetland Islands cannot be registered as a Shetland in the United States today. This is because the original island pony and the American Shetland are now so different.

The American Shetland is a high-strung show horse. Notice the long hooves on this champion stallion. USDA PHOTO

The Welsh Pony has natural grace and beauty, even when standing still. USDA PHOTO

The Welsh Pony

The Welsh Pony is a beautiful, ancient breed that came from the rugged mountains of Wales. These animals have long, full manes and tails. They look very much like small Arabians. Some say that Arabian stallions escaped from the wrecked ships of the Spanish Armada. Then they came ashore in Wales and bred with the native wild ponies. This produced the elegant Welsh Pony of today.

Welsh Ponies in the United States come in two sizes. The smaller ponies are no more than 12 hands high. In Britain, these smaller ponies are called "Welsh Mountain Ponies." The larger ponies, which are from 12 to 13.2 hands, are called "Welsh Ponies." In the United States, both sizes of ponies are simply called "Welsh Ponies," and animals up to 14.2 hands are acceptable. Whatever their size, Welsh Ponies are gentle, hardy animals. The larger ponies are fine mounts for children up to sixteen years old. They are used as small pleasure horses and also as jumpers for children.

Welsh Ponies were once shown like Shetlands in the United States. Their hooves were grown long and were weighted with heavy shoes, and their tails were set in an arched position. Their bodies were stretched out when shown, like those of Shetlands. But now Welsh Pony breeders appreciate the natural beauty of their animals. Young ponies are shown without any shoes at all, and older ones can also be shoeless. They are allowed to stand naturally, and their own graceful "floating trot" is used instead of a forced high-stepping gait when they are shown in harness.

Pony of the Americas

The Pony of the Americas (POA) is among the newer breeds of horses. The breed was begun in 1954 as a small pleasure horse especially for children. Before the POA came along, there was no western-style pony for kids. The name Pony of the Americas was chosen because many of the first breeding ponies came from Mexico and South America. POAs have Appaloosa coloring and are from 11.2 to 13.2 hands high. They are bred for gentleness as well as for color since they are designed to be used by children. POAs were first pro-

This Pony of the Americas shows fine Appaloosa traits. Notice its spotted coat and the white sclera of its eye. BILL MUNOZ

duced by breeding Appaloosas with Shetland or Welsh Ponies. Arabians and Quarter Horses are also important in POA breeding. The ideal POA looks like a small Arabian-Quarter Horse cross.

The POA is very popular; there are about 25,000 registered ponies. The gaits of the POA are smoother than those of Shetland Ponies. POAs are easier to get along with than many Shetlands. In POA shows, most of the events are strictly for children. But POAs are also popular with small adults, for a small horse eats less food and needs less space than a large one. It is also more comfortable for a small person to ride. To be a registered POA, a pony must have at least one POA parent and must show Appaloosa traits.

Two Chincoteague Ponies challenge one another in the confines of a corral on Pony Penning Day. ALAN J. KANIA

Chincoteague Ponies

A small island named Assatcague, off the coast of northern Virginia, is home to the Chincoteague Pony. These famous ponies have lived wild on the islands for over 300 years. They live a hard life. In the summer it is hot, and biting sand flies force the ponies to wade into the water until only their heads are above the surface. In the winter big storms come with cold, biting winds. Every year these ponies are driven through the water to the island of Chincoteague, where most of the foals are auctioned off. If the foals were not removed, there would soon be too many ponies for the tough island grasses to feed.

The Chincoteague Ponies were once mostly solid colors. But in modern times Shetland, Welsh, and pinto ponies were let loose on the island, and today pintos are especially common. The ponies are usually 12 to 13.2 hands high. They have long, thick manes and tails. When the foals are tamed and trained, they make very good ponies for children to ride.

Tiny Tim is only 19″ tall. Unlike Tiny Tim, most American Miniature Horses are perfectly proportioned. COURTESY OF C. M. BOND

Miniature Horses

People like tiny animals, and horses are no exception. Many horse breeders in the United States concentrate on raising American Miniature Horses. Even though they are small, these horses are not called ponies. They must be no more than 8.2 hands high. Many of them are even smaller. The first miniature horses in the United States were used in the coal mines of Virginia in the late 1800s. Now they are mostly backyard pets. Miniature horses are also shown pulling tiny wagons in parades and fairs.

Miniature horses may be small, but they are like bigger horses in other ways. The tiny stallions try to fight with one another, and the little mares take good care of their foals. Some miniatures are like stocky little draft horses, while others are built more like Thorough-breds.

CHAPTER SEVEN
At Work and at Play

Even in our machine age, people still use horses for many different purposes. In addition to draft horses which work on the farm, there are still cow ponies which work on the cattle ranch. People enjoy training animals to work in flat racing, harness racing, and flashy horse shows. But they also like to train horses for polo games, jumping contests, and rodeos. Without the help of horses, none of these exciting events could take place.

Polo is an exciting but expensive sport. HERB BYERS, INTERNATIONAL MUSEUM OF THE HORSE

Polo

Polo may be the world's oldest game. It was played perhaps 3,000 years ago in Persia. Modern polo is played on a field 300 yards long and 200 yards wide. There are two teams of four players. The players use T-shaped sticks to hit a small, hard ball between goalposts at either end of the field. This kind of polo is popular on the east and west coasts. It is a very expensive sport. A player must have three to five horses to ride in each game because the fast racing towards the ball is tiring for the horses. And since the horses become very hot and sweaty, someone else must also be around to walk each horse until it has cooled off.

Another sort of polo is popular in parts of the west and in Florida. This is called cowboy polo. There are five members to each cowboy polo team. The cowboy polo field is smaller than the standard polo field. With more players and a smaller field, each rider needs only one horse. The field is dirt rather than grass so it is less expensive to take care of. A large rubber ball is used which moves freely over the rough surface of the field. Cowboy polo has some rules of its own too. In standard polo, the players must go for the ball. They must try to keep their horses apart. But in cowboy polo, some of the fun comes from using the horses against one another. One horse can lean on another and push it as far as three feet without penalty.

Cowboy polo is a less expensive, more rough-and-tumble version of this ancient game. COURTESY OF JIM COLE

The term "polo pony" is confusing since today's polo mount is usually a full-sized horse. Thoroughbreds and Thoroughbred crosses are popular in standard polo, while Quarter Horses arc often used in cowboy polo. But for either sport, the horse must be able to run fast and turn quickly. It must enjoy competition and not be afraid of sticks, balls, or other horses. Polo requires an especially tough, all-around kind of horse.

Jumping

Jumping horses is a very popular sport. Many horse shows have jumping events, and there are shows just for jumping. With this sport, the only thing that matters is how well the horse can get over a fence. The horse can be any breed or any mixture of breeds. It doesn't have to be pretty. It can be small or large. It can jump gracefully or awkwardly. But it must jump well.

Rider Terry Rudd is a top-ranked American competitor. NATIONAL HORSE SHOW

The jumping course has several turns and several different fences. Some of the jumps are higher than others and some are wider. There are two sorts of jumping contests. In one, the horse and rider go over the course twice. On the first round, the horse must make every jump without knocking off the rails of any fences. The second round is timed so faster horses will do better. In the other kind of contest, horses also lose points if their hooves touch the top rail of any fence. If more than one horse makes it cleanly through the round, the jumps are raised for the next round and so forth, until one horse wins.

There are also three kinds of horse races that take place on a jumping course—the point-to-point race, the hurdling race, and the true steeplechase.

In a point-to-point race, only certain "points" along the race are marked. The race takes place over fences in open country.

A hurdling race is shorter than a steeplechase. The fences are lower and there are fewer fences in each mile. A hurdle race requires at least four jumps per mile, while a steeplechase requires at least six.

The steeplechase is the biggest and most exciting jumping race. Each jump must be at least four-and-a-half feet high and three feet wide. The jumps are made of brush or shrubs. There also must be a water jump which is at least twelve feet wide. Another required obstacle is a five-foot wide ditch with fences at each

Close competition adds excitement in this point-to-point race.
DOUGLAS LEES, NATIONAL STEEPLECHASE AND HUNT ASSOCIATION

end. Horses often fall at steeplechases, and sometimes horses or riders are hurt. Thoroughbreds are generally used for these races.

.70.

Hunting

A horse can be a hunter without ever going on a hunt. The term "hunter" refers to horses that are used in fox hunting. But it is also used for horses which compete in hunter classes at horse shows. Hunter classes are a kind of jumping contest. The horses are not only judged on how cleanly they go over the jumps. They are also rated on their form as they jump and on the way in which they approach the jumps. In hunter classes, the jumps themselves are supposed to be more natural than in jumping events. They are supposed to look more like the kinds of obstacles a horse would come across in a fox hunt. Hunters must be big strong horses, so draft horses

Fox hunting with hounds is popular in the northeastern part of the United States. Here Mrs. John Glass is all set to go in the Norfolk Hunt, Dover, Massachusetts. WENDY DAVIS

are sometimes crossed with other breeds such as Thoroughbreds to produce hunters.

Fox hunting is an old English sport which is popular in some parts of the eastern United States as well. When a fox became a nuisance to farmers by attacking his chickens, the fox hunters would run down the fox and capture it. Dogs called foxhounds are used to track the fox. People on horseback run after the dogs, jumping over fences and streams to keep up. When the fox is caught and killed, its tail is given to the rider who wins the hunt. In some horse shows, there are special hunter classes for horses which have actually done hunting with hounds.

Cowboys on horseback still herd cattle in western states like Colorado. ALAN J. KANIA

Cow Ponies

Many people think that the days of the cow pony are over. But these tough and well-trained horses are still used all across the western states. Some ranchers use motorcycles to herd their cattle, but most still rely on horses to do the work. Quarter Horses are the most popular cattle horses. But Arabians, Morgans, Appaloosas, and even Saddlebreds are favored by some ranchers. A rancher's children may even help in a roundup while riding their POAs. Many cow ponies are "just plain horses" too.

Cow ponies must be able to work long hours without getting tired. They must feel at home around cattle, and they must understand the wishes of their riders quickly. A good cow horse can understand which cow its rider wants to separate from the herd and will know how to cut the cow out. This "cutting horse" skill is tested in western horse shows in special classes. A truly good cutting horse takes three years to train and is worth a lot of money.

Barrel racing is a rodeo sport for women and girls which requires well-trained horses. BILL MUNOZ

Bronc riding is one of the most popular rodeo events. HOWARD SKAGGS

Rodeo Horses

Rodeos began as contests between cowboys to see who could perform a cowhand's jobs the best. In the old days, cowboys needed to ride unbroken bucking horses until they calmed down. They had to rope cattle on the run. They needed to wrestle calves to the ground before branding. All these skills may not be needed by today's cowboy, but they are still tested in the modern rodeo. Other events which provide excitement have been added too.

Some rodeo horses are well-trained animals. The calf roper's horse must be able to run straight and fast until the cowboy throws his lasso at the calf. The horse

.75.

slows down as the lasso flies through the air. When the lasso catches the calf, the horse must pull the rope gently back. He pulls until the rope is tight enough to keep the calf down while the cowboy ties its legs. The horse must do all these things on its own since the cowboy is busy with his part of the job.

The bulldoggers, who wrestle cattle to the ground after chasing them on horseback, also need highly trained mounts. Rodeos often feature a man or woman who does fancy tricks on horseback, such as somersaults or juggling. The trick rider's horse must know its routines perfectly.

But some rodeo horses are valued for their lack of training—the bucking broncs. These animals do not like to have humans on their backs and will do whatever they can to get a rider off. Some broncs hump up in the middle and jump up and down with stiff legs. Others fling their heels high in the air, trying to send the rider flying over their heads. Each horse has its own bucking style. A bronc which is especially difficult to ride earns the respect of all the rodeo cowboys.

Horses have always been important in our country. They helped people explore and settle the land. They still work on farms and ranches. And they help people enjoy life by providing exciting competition, pleasant riding, and loving friendship. Because of their strength, loyalty, and beauty, horses will continue to play important roles in human life.

Suggested Reading

Glenn Balch, *The Book of Horses* (Four Winds, N.Y., 1967)

Irene Brady, *America's Horses and Ponies* (Houghton Mifflin, Boston, 1969)

Barbara Ford and Ronald R. Keiper, *The Island Ponies: An Environmental Study of their Life on Assateague* (Morrow, N.Y., 1979)

Marguerite Henry, *All About Horses* (Random House, N.Y., 1962)

Robert Hofsinde, *The Indian and His Horse* (Morrow, N.Y., 1960)

Bob Krueger, *The Wild Mustangs* (McKay, N.Y., 1980)

Sigmund A. Lavine and Brigid Casey, *Wonders of Ponies* (Dodd Mead, N.Y., 1980)

Jack Denton Scott and Ozzie Sweet, *Island of Wild Horses* (Putnam, N.Y., 1978)

Louis Taylor, *The Story of America's Horses* (World, N.Y., 1968)

Neil Thompson, *A Closer Look at Horses* (Franklin Watts, N.Y., 1978)

Glossary

albino: An animal with no brown pigment (coloring). An albino's fur is white and its eyes are pink because they have no coloring. The pink in the eyes comes from tiny blood vessels in the iris of the eye.

Barb: An old breed of small desert horses from North Africa. Barbs do not have a dished face as Arabians do.

bay: A bay horse has a body which is some shade of red, from golden red to dark mahogany red. Its mane, tail, and lower legs are black.

breed association: An organization which sets standards for a particular breed of horses, such as Arabian, Belgian, and so on. The breed association also keeps track of the individual horses of the breed (see register).

brood mare: A mare (female horse) which is used for breeding purposes rather than for showing or racing. Brood mares can have one foal each year.

chestnut: A horse with a reddish coat. The mane, legs, and tail may be the same shade as the body, lighter, or darker, but never black.

colt: Usually, a young male horse. A young female is called a filly. Sometimes, however, the word "colts" is used generally to describe all young horses.

conquistador: A Spanish conqueror of Peru and Mexico during the 16th century.

cutting horse: A horse trained to separate individual cows from a herd; it "cuts" them out of the herd.

foal: A young horse.

gait: One of the ways an animal can move. The walk, trot, canter, and gallop are the common gaits of the horse.

gelding: A male horse whose testes (organs which produce sperm and male hormones) have been removed. Geldings are less excitable than stallions and make excellent riding and work horses.

hand: The measurement used for the height of a horse. A hand is equal to four inches. The horse's height is measured from the ground to the top of the withers (shoulders).

Hispaniola: An island in the West Indies. Today, Hispaniola is divided into two countries, Haiti and the Dominican Republic.

lasso: The rope used by a cowboy to catch cattle.

mane: The long, coarse hair which grows along the top of a horse's neck.

mare: A female horse.

mottled: Marked by patches of two colors mixed up together.

mustang: A horse living wild in America whose ancestors were tame horses which escaped or were set free.

pony: A small horse less than 14.2 hands tall.

purebred: A horse whose parents both belonged to the same breed.

rack: A gait in which each foot is set down separately. Only a few breeds of horses can do the rack, and they must be taught by their trainers.

register: To list a horse officially with a breed association. When a horse is registered, information such as the name of the parents, the date of birth, color, and any distinctive markings must be listed.

roan: A roan horse has white hairs mixed up with hairs of another color in its coat. For example, a strawberry roan has a mixture of red-and-white hairs.

rodeo: A show in which cowboys compete at riding bucking horses and bulls, roping cattle, and other ranching skills.

sclera: The portion of the eye which surrounds the iris.

sorrel: A light, golden-red-colored (light chestnut) horse. Sorrels often have white or light-colored manes and tails.

stallion: A male horse which is not a gelding.

steer: A male cow which has been castrated (had its testes removed).

stock horse: A horse trained to work with cattle.

trail riding: Riding cross-country and through the woods along trails. When people compete in trail rides, the condition of the horse at the end of the ride is important as well as the time it took to get from the start to the finish.

trot: The natural gait of a horse which is between a walk and a run.

withers: The top of a horse's shoulders. The withers make a small hump right at the base of the horse's neck just behind its front legs.

Index